JOHN B

From the author of T

PIECE *of* CAKE

A Simple Guide
to Starting a Church, a Ministry or Other Life Projects

ISBN-13: 978-1491292136

ISBN-10: 149129213X

Published by Significant Publishing

Printed in the United States of America

To my children, Skylar, Parker, Jet, Ella and Eva.
You absolutely can succeed in the assignments God gives you!

john burton

is a church planter, conference speaker and author with a mandate to see the fire of God's presence invade cities and nations. He planted Revolution Church in Manitou Springs, Colorado and Revival Church in Detroit, Michigan.

John's ministry style could be described as wildly passionate, engaging, humorous and loaded with the flow and power of the Holy Spirit.

The prevailing theme of the ministry God has given John revolves around the topic of encountering God. Where God is, things happen. In His presence, the place where He is, is the fullness of joy. As we discover the wonderful mystery of walking in the Spirit, praying always and making aggressive strides in faith, life becomes incredible!

It truly is an experience in the invisible realm. As we tangibly experience God through deep and active prayer we are interacting *in the Spirit*. As we walk by faith and understand how amazing a Holy Spirit driven life is, being a Christian believer quickly becomes the greatest adventure on earth!

John is currently focused on teaching, consulting, writing and ministering to churches.

If you would like to invite John to speak at your church, conference, camp or other event, please visit johnburton.net.

CONTENTS

PIECE of CAKE

A Simple Guide to Starting a Church, a Ministry or Other Life Project

Introduction
An Apostolic Freak

I often feel like a freak in the Kingdom. Not because I don't fit in, or because I don't have great friends and connections in the ministry. But, rather, because I'm continually provoked by the possibilities to change the world through various ministries, projects and endeavors—and that results in a lot of action, shifting, trial and error that takes many beyond their comfort zones. As a visionary, my heart is to provoke and awaken a generation to the greatness of God, and I am seeking any and every vehicle I can find, or invent, to get that message out there.

Apostolic people are pioneers who go where no man had dared to go before. They tear down, plant and build. God is awakening leaders today who fear nothing and respond immediately to his commands to shock the planet with the fire of his Spirit! This lifestyle will trouble the status quo and irritate the hesitant.

God is looking for people to blaze a new trail—people who won't delay, and who won't wait for others to affirm them with a vigorous thumb's up. He is seeking people, like Paul, who have the confidence to run the race and call people to follow them as they follow Christ.

I had a striking vision one day that clearly explains what God is doing in this apostolic age. I was walking with thousands of other Christians down a clear, well packed dirt path. We were marching toward the horizon together. These people were legitimate Believers who were following Jesus as many others had before them. Along the left side of the path was very thick forest.

As I was walking with everybody else, I was startled as I heard a distinct, "Psssst!" coming from the woods. I heard it again and then turned and looked at the edge of the trail along side the trees. I saw Jesus standing there, but he didn't look very much like the picture we all have in our minds when we think of him. He reminded me more of Peter Pan!

He was youthful, jumping up and down, with excitement in his eyes. He was thrilled that he got my attention! He had a machete in his hand and simply said, "Hey! Follow me!"

He went running into the thick, dark jungle, swinging his machete. I couldn't resist, so I looked at my friends who were walking with me and said, "Come on! Follow me! I'm following Jesus!"

I ran into the woods and saw a youthful, intently focused Jesus well ahead swinging his machete, blazing a trail. He stopped for a moment and turned around and was elated when he saw my friends and me following him. He was jumping and laughing and chopping away every hindering branch and vine. My heart was pounding as I found myself running directly behind Jesus himself as he led into a mysterious new adventure.

The vision ended there. God immediately said to me, "The

clear, well defined path you and the thousands of others were on in the beginning of the vision was once a dense, nearly impenetrable forest like the one Jesus was creating a brand new trail through. A clear path that impacted the masses started as a rough, nondescript path. Will you leave the familiar, beaten path of yesterday and lead others into exhilarating, liberating, fresh new ministries?

Of course, I said yes!

I wasn't prepared. I didn't have full understanding—but I had to be instant. I had to blaze that new trail no matter who followed and no matter how lonely and vulnerable I felt.

I've patterned my entire ministry and life after that vision. I've succeeded some and failed often. This book will help you come alive in that process as you refuse to hesitate when God calls you to start new ministries, churches, projects or other endeavors.

Some of my successes and failures in starting ministries and projects include:

- A regional youth gathering in Dayton, Ohio
- A park ministry in Dayton, Ohio
- Developing a youth ministry in San Diego, California
- Developing a youth ministry in Dallas, Texas
- Writing several books
- Revolution Church in Manitou Springs, Colorado
- A regional prayer ministry in Colorado Springs, Colorado
- A regional prayer ministry in Detroit, Michigan
- A ministry school in Detroit, Michigan
- Revival Church North in Washington, Michigan
- Directing the Intro to IHOP internship at the International House of Prayer in Kansas City, Missouri
- An online ministry school based in Detroit, Michigan
- Gathering one thousand intercessors in Detroit, Michigan
- Training 10/40 Window leaders in Thailand
- A graphic and web design business

And there are many more. As I relive these adventures through writing this book, it's exciting! I have failed often, and have come off ridiculously at times, but I'm thrilled that it doesn't impact me enough to keep me from trying again! Read on if you dare move off the beaten path and onto your own dark, jungle trail!

Chapter One
The Laborers Are Few!

People are longing to launch into ministry, and to initiate ministries and projects—and this is good! We are living in an era when the Lord is vigilantly identifying critical end-time ministries and the laborers who will give leadership to them. I am regularly contacted by zealous men and women of God who know they have been tapped by God to make a difference, yet are unsure about how to take the leap into ministry.

This uncertainty results in dreams and desires that feel like little more than a vapor of gasoline that's unable to get the engine started. The hope gets deferred and the heart gets sick. I can't even count the number of potential Earth shakers who are experiencing defeat without even making an attempt at success! Fear of failure results in actual failure!

Whether you are starting a church or a ministry, an important life project or even a minor endeavor, the message is the same: Get started! Starting a ministry that is birthed by God is truly much simpler than you may realize—it's a piece of cake! And, there's icing on the cake! And there's fire on top of that!

When I am awakened to a fresh ministry idea, I'm instantly invigorated. Often, I will actually begin developing the ministry immediately—within hours or minutes! It's important to let the vision activate and gain traction immediately upon conception.

I'll share one example with you that should make what I'm trying to explain extremely easy to understand. This book in your hands is a case in point. A couple of weeks ago I felt impressed that a book like this would benefit people who are being drawn into ministry. I let the vision for this project activate internally as I pondered it. Then, I put it on the shelf without giving it much more thought at all, until this afternoon when I had some free time and another urge to get this resource developed. Around 2pm I started designing the book cover (I'm also a graphic designer) and completed it by 5pm. After playing some games with my wife and the kids in the back yard, I went to my office and started outlining the book at around 7pm. The words you are reading right now were written at 9:02pm. The point? I got started. I didn't need the stars to align correctly or for an angel to arrive with a scroll containing a freshly written outline from Heaven for me to use. I didn't need to wait to become a premier expert in this subject or to receive affirmation from others about this project. I refused to allow any excuse to artificially magnify a simple project into an insurmountable task. The job wasn't overwhelming in the least. All I had to do was write. That's something I learned to do in elementary school, so I was qualified.

If I didn't believe this book had at least some eternal value, it wouldn't matter when I started or finished it. However, if lives are hanging in the balance, if ministries are awaiting a catalytic charge to help get them off the ground and if people are waiting to experience the power and love of Jesus that will be expressed through those ministries, I simply had to excuse every argument against my mandate out of my mind and begin.

Also, just because I have already logged years in ministry as a laborer planting churches, preaching and serving does not mean I am fulfilling my quota of labor. There is truly much work to be done and when God drops a project into my spirit, the only delay that is permitted is that of his timing. The labor must be completed, and if we understood the supernatural adrenaline rush that comes from advancing in ministry and impacting lives, we would never delay again!

A Simple First Step

This book will either be my seventh or eighth, depending on whether I finish this one or another I'm writing at the same time, *The Coming Church*, first. Nearly a decade ago I had yet to write a book, but I did have quite a bit burning in me—messages of transformation. God knew those messages had to come out of me, and he helped me take the first simple step toward writing my first book.

I was living and leading a church in Manitou Springs, Colorado at that time. I decided to head into a secluded part of the Rocky Mountains for a night of prayer and fasting, and while little of significance seemed to happen that night, the Lord did give me an assignment. As I was sitting on the bed that night, after an evening of uninspired boredom, God presented me with a simple project—he instructed me to write, to journal, for the next year. I had never kept a journal before, and I didn't know why he wanted me to start. Maybe something significant was going to happen in the church and he wanted me to be a ready writer, recording everything as it happened? I did not know, but I did begin to write.

I wrote most every day, and, trust me, you really don't want to read most of what I wrote. You see, hindsight has revealed to me that the purpose of that project was not to record a great move of God or to one day see that journal published and sitting on the same bookstore shelf as *The Diary of Anne Frank*. It was simply to get me comfortable writing.

Here are a few of my journal entries:

PREFACE

This is the beginning of a one-year journey. Actually, the journey I'm on started long ago—but I've been prompted by the Spirit of God to focus, to highlight, to dive deep into the trials and victories and revelations of my life each day for the next year.

The purpose you ask? I want to leave a legacy for my family.

The Lord did something quite amazing in my life recently. I was in prayer and I was experiencing a strong presence of the Lord. He told me that he's pleased with me and that I'm going deeper into his presence. I was excited! God was pleased and I was going deeper! Then the Lord surprised me. He told me that if I wanted to go deeper that I had to take every area of my life with me. God challenged me. I have to take my wife and kids with me—into the deep, challenging, overwhelming presence of God. My thought life has to go too. My entertainment life, my social life, my self-discipline. They all go with me. So, that is my commission. What you hold in your hand is nothing more than a devotional, a record of my life for the next year. I do pray, however, this devotional effectively displays the overwhelming staying power of the Holy Spirit. I pray a strong anointing and very clear picture into the heart of man and the heart of God. As an old song goes, "Great things happen when God mixes with man!" What you will experience as you begin the journey with me are my passions, my dreams, my questions, and most certainly God's answers.

I pray as this is read by my wife Amy, my children Skylar and Parker and any yet to come that they would be drawn deeper into the presence of God. It's really, really good there!

Noah built an ark and he saved his household. This devotional is one plank in our ark. Salvation is one of the keys. There is joy in the salvation of Jesus Christ! There is abundant life. There is peace. There is purpose. There is confidence. You won't only witness miracles- you will initiate them! Your life will demand miracles for survival. Why? Because we're going where we've never been before. We're crossing the Jordan River into a new world—a Promised Land that is full of blessing yet full of resistant enemies. These giants are about to be confronted and devastated by the miraculous power of God himself!

Amy, Skylar, Parker and anyone else that has chosen to join me on my Journey- simply know that God is with us always, the impossible is probable and we will be dangerous weapons in the hands of our mighty God!
Let's possess the land!

DAY ONE
Fri Dec 20, 2002

I decided to begin today instead of waiting until the first of the year so I can give this devotional to my wife and kids as a Christmas present next year. As you begin with me, simply begin here, regardless of the date, and follow along.

I am writing this first page in a tiny cabin at Praise Mountain in the Rocky Mountains outside of Florissant, Colorado. This is a prayer and fasting retreat dedicated to the spiritual health of ministers and other believers. I am listening to a worship song that goes, "I am hungry, I am hungry, I am hungry for more of You." I actually found myself singing, "I am hungry, I am hungry, I am hungry for Taco Bell!"

The Lord has been refreshing me to amazing degrees lately. Pastoring our new church plant (Revolution Church in Manitou Springs, CO.) is a Promised Land experience. Excitement, blessing, miracles, promise, adventure and enemies everywhere! John 10:10 is often separated into two halves:

1. The thief does not come except to steal, kill and destroy.
2. But I have come that they may have life and have it more abundantly.

I believe we can become unbalanced, and susceptible to the enemy, if we focus on one half of the verse over the other. The enemy is there and hates us. But, in the midst of that-through prayer and battles and focus and surrender to God, we will have abundant life.

So, my heart today shouts this:

- Don't underestimate the power of the enemy.
- Don't overestimate the power of the enemy.
- Don't underestimate our responsibility to be full of the power of Jesus Christ so we can engage and defeat the enemy!

Here's a quote I heard tonight as I listened to a tape of one of my favorite speakers, Glen Berteau:

"We must refuse to live a life, to face a circumstance, or to be in a situation without changing it."

I love you Amy, Skylar and Parker.

DAY EIGHTY FIVE
Mon Mar 10, 2003

You know, though I live an exciting life and am creative and absolutely love to be spontaneous, I think I'm a pretty boring guy on Monday. I slept in, played with the kids and went for our standard Chinese fare for lunch. I know the kids love this 'boring' part of my life. They love to wrestle with me, go to the buffet, go to the store and watch, "The Wiggles" on TV. (Yes, it's true, I love The Wiggles!)

Well, I know my boys will remember these wonderful times for years and years to come. I can remember as far back to three years of age. I was looking at the window of the hospital room where my brother was being born. I was with my dad. We then went to a little amusement park for the afternoon. I loved Daddy Day too.

DAY THREE HUNDRED FIFTY TWO
Mon December 1, 2003

I can't believe I'm coming to the end of this journal! It's been a great thing to do, though I've discovered I'm not a "journaler." It's tough to do it sometimes!

But, the continuing works of God are so sweet and worth documenting. We had an excellent meeting with Pastor Ted and some of the other Secret Prayer leaders Monday. We heard testimonies of what God had done in the churches we visited and are excited about continuing the church to church prayer events.

We're currently looking for some strong leadership to step into position at the church. I feel very impressed that God's helping us up to the next level, slowly and gently. We'll see a strong foundation become stronger and healthier.

Clearly, the information I was recording in the journal during that year was not of much value for anybody but my family and me, and possibly our church family at the time, but the project was important. I heard from God one night and began immediately. He was training me as a laborer to be instant as a writer, as one who would communicate messages to a generation that was he was also preparing for service. Since then, I am continually writing articles for my website, books, teachings and other mediums. Rarely does a day go by that something doesn't burn in me and out of me onto Facebook, Twitter, into a sermon or an outline in preparation for another book.

Interestingly, Anne Frank was much more perceptive than I was when she realized her journal entries provided an opportunity to change the world in which she lived. She decided to rewrite her original, personal journal and prepare it for publication just after hearing a speech on the radio by the Dutch Cabinet Minister Gerritt Bolkestein on March 28, 1944:

"History cannot be written on the basis of official decisions and documents alone. If our descendants are to understand fully what we as a nation have had to endure and overcome during these years, then what we really need are ordinary documents -- a diary, letters from a worker in Germany, a collection of sermons given by a parson or priest. Not until we succeed in bringing together vast quantities of this simple, everyday material will the picture of our struggle for freedom be painted in its full depth and glory."

A few years after I had finished my journal, I started receiving very interesting prophetic words about the call for me to write books, and prayerfully, change the world in which I live. So, one day in the prayer room God rocked me with a message on revival based on Acts chapter two. Immediately, as I was burning with that message, I grabbed a marker and developed a raw outline on the whiteboard, and shortly after that I completed my first book, *20 Elements of Revival.* The rest then followed.

I knew there would be many arguments that would keep me from pumping out the messages as fast as I received them. Perfectionism was not an option. While I always embrace a spirit of excellence, I determined then that I would not attempt to edit the books perfectly. I wasn't concerned about much else than getting it printed and into the hands of the people God wanted to read it. As you will see as you read the rest of this quickly developed book, I follow the same principles in every other area of my ministry. There is much to be done, and you and I are assigned a significant portion of it. The world awaits.

Chapter Two
Sweet Failure!

Success doesn't develop experts nearly as well as failure does. Thomas Edison said, "I have not failed 10,000 times. I have not failed once. I have succeeded in proving that those 10,000 ways will not work. When I have eliminated the ways that will not work, I will find the way that will work." *(attributed to Thomas Edison)*

Edison, when queried by a reporter about the seemingly incredible difficulties associated with his work on the lightbulb rebutted, "I have not failed 700 times. I've succeeded in proving 700 ways how not to build a lightbulb." *(attributed to Thomas Edison)*

If we understand the scope of our project, it's actually quite insane to presume we will accomplish it without significant and repeated failures.

In fact, the inventors of the famed lubricant WD-40 were so unintimidated by failure, that they actually included it in the name of their product. If you knew you'd fail thirty-nine times and succeed one, would you proceed?

From WD40.com:

In 1953, a fledgling company called Rocket Chemical Company and its staff of three set out to create a line of rust-prevention solvents and degreasers for use in the aerospace industry, in a small lab in San Diego, California. It took them 40 attempts to get the water displacing formula worked out. But they must have been really good, because the original secret formula for WD–40®—which stands for Water Displacement perfected on the 40th try—is still in use today. *(quoted from www.wd40.com)*

Yes, you are going to fail. Go ahead and wrestle with it now, you can't avoid it. I don't mean ultimate failure, of course. But, I do mean that you will pray much, do your best to gain insight from God, consider your best options, seek wisdom from others and then move out with at least a measure of confidence—and you will experience failure!

Thomas Edison could have named his light bulb, Light-bulb–1000! Maybe you can name the church you are considering planting First Church–100! Failure should not intimidate you! People will presume you to be inadequate, confused or immature during your experimenting.

Most young ministers crave for others to see them as successful and steady with a pipeline directly into the command center of Heaven. The reality? We see in part. We understand little. We have clarity on a small part of the big picture, and when we initiate action, others will watch as we stumble and struggle. Are you OK with that?

Thomas Edison said, "Just because something doesn't do what you planned it to do doesn't mean it's useless." (*Quoted in Artifacts: An Archaeologist's Year in Silicon Valley (2001) by Christine Finn. p. 90*)

Your job is not to be so careful that you avoid failure, it's to be instant in obedience! In fact, failure is sweet when you learn how to handle the pressure it brings. Failure is an effective and desirable teacher. You may actually find yourself enjoying the various failures you experience, as a researcher would in a laboratory, in your pursuit toward efficiency and success. Really, the main thing standing in the way of the sweetness of failure is pride. If our goal is to impress people instead of developing ministries that set them free, we have no business even considering entering into a ministry project. We need to mature a little bit more first.

I stumbled across a blog article that I thought was interesting. It does a good job of explaining how to quickly initiate and develop a project:

> "We only win in the long run by getting out there and bloodied in the short run." *(attributed to Tom Peters)*

> This blog is an example of rapid prototyping.

> One week ago this blog did not exist except for a few ideas in my head so I thought it would be helpful to show how I went from step one to launch for very little time and money.

> Now I own about 25 film books to every business book I have, but I think I first learned about rapid prototyping from Tom Peters. Some have called Thomas Edison "the father of prototyping," but I imagine it goes back to a time closer to starting the first fire or inventing the wheel.

> What is rapid prototyping? In filmmaking terms, it's Edward Burns having a meeting at the end of 2010 with the Tribeca Film Festival people and coming up with an idea that he should make a feature to show for the festival's 10th year and a few months later the film is written, cast, shot, edited and premiered. In an industry where the typical film can be in development for 3 to 5 years before it gets produced (or dies in development) Burns' Newlyweds is definitely prototyping. Sylvester Stallone writing Rocky in six days is an example of rapid prototyping.

> In the manufacturing world, a team of people may be put in charge of a project to design a widget quickly to meet a need in the marketplace. Rapid prototyping is messy business as

it tends to follow the motto "fail early, fail often." Because in the failing is where breakthroughs happen. *(Scott W. Smith, efilmmaking.wordpress.com)*

It's always at least a little interesting hearing about someone else's failures, and how they grew through them. When my wife and I moved to Colorado Springs to begin the process of starting a church, we honestly had no idea what we were doing. We didn't have any money set aside for our church plant and we weren't sent out by an organization. It was simply a boots on the ground venture. We showed up and started into the trial and error process.

One of our first steps was to connect with the largest church in the area, a ministry that we absolutely loved. They had a massive, vibrant small group ministry, and we thought it would be good to at least connect there as we waited for clarity on when to actually start the church. So, we attended the small group leader training and started planning our new small group. We were excited! We weren't starting our own church yet, but we didn't care. We wanted to connect with some new friends who shared our values, and we wanted to support the ministry of that church.

The weekend of the huge ministry fair came. This is where small group leaders were given a booth somewhere on the campus of the church where people could stop by before and after the Sunday services and get information about the various groups. Our booth was one of the best! We had looping video, excellent information and a powerful vision. It felt like a slam dunk!

Well, since this chapter is about failure, you know what's coming! We were given one of the rooms in the church to hold our small group meeting as we hadn't gotten settled in our own home yet. We prepared for the group and arrived early to setup.

When it was about 6:45pm, we had expected at least a few people to arrive early, but nobody did. At 6:55pm, we peeked down the long hallway to see how many people were walking toward our room. There were none. At straight up 7pm, Amy and I started to feel sadness rolling in, and by 7:15pm our dreams were fully crushed. At 7:30pm we packed up and snuck out with our tails between our legs, defeated.

We mustered up the courage to do the same thing the following week, just in case some people got the news of our amazing group a little late. This time by 7:05pm, we exited the building and went out for a lonely dinner, just Amy and me. Sweet failure didn't feel so sweet that night. The group ended as fast as it started.

But, of course, we could not give up—though we did adjust our sails. We ended up launching Revolution Church a while later in our small living room with our family and a couple of other new friends. From there we grew into a 700 square foot building which held around 25 people, and then into a 2,000 square foot building where we peaked at 70, and finally into a 20,000 square foot building where we regularly ran around 100 in a very difficult region that was steeped in the occult. You see, in Manitou Springs, Colorado, at least 14 churches have started and failed in their first two years since the 1980's. Revolution Church thrived.

Missing God

One of the most prevalent issues that I come across on a regular basis as I talk to emerging leaders is the fear of missing God. Often people feel led to initiate a ministry, or to make a move in that direction, but they are afraid of being outside of God's plan. This is a legitimate concern, but fear should not drive us. Wisdom should.

There was a time when I was living the life as a youth pastor in a church in the San Diego area. It was amazing! I was at the beach every Thursday and had a stress free, invigorating position in the church. I had full liberty to develop the youth department according to my vision and ideas. After a year and a half in that church I was offered a position in a large church in the Dallas area. It was a completely different environment, and making such a move would be a huge decision. I felt I had confirmation and I was excited about the possibilities this new opportunity presented, but I was afraid of missing God.

A good friend of mine gave me some of the simplest yet most profound and life changing advice I had ever received. He simply quoted scripture and said, "The steps of a righteous man are ordered of the Lord."

The revelation was instant. If I was living a righteous life, and was making righteous decisions, God would order my steps—even if and when I made a misstep! The fear and pressure of making a right versus a wrong decision lifted off of me! I have used that counsel countless times in my life since. When I feel led to make a decision, I ensure I'm living in righteousness and am doing my due diligence through prayer and seeking counsel, and then I step! I trust that God will direct my steps, and if I'm off track a little bit, he will lovingly guide me back. It's really a glorious way to live!

As I do this, I am fully confident that a lot of sweet failure is ahead of me, and I learn how to stay joyful and teachable as I learn from every ministry experiment.

Keep in mind, I am not advising a haphazard life. That will only cause you unnecessary frustration. Measure your decisions and step according to wisdom as you live in the spirit, and refuse to fear knowing that both temporary failures and ultimate victory are both ahead!

I've heard it said that we should make quick, pretty good decisions as opposed to calculated, perfect ones. Using this book as an example, I could have pulled out various resources, created a perfect outline, pondered it for a few months and eventually start writing. But, instead, my quick, pretty good decision has resulted in writing chapter two just one day after I started designing and writing the book. If my schedule allows, I can have this entire book written, in less than perfect but fully acceptable form, in just a few days! I'm literally sitting here in the prayer room unsure of what I will write next, but that's OK. My goal is to pour out my heart, get the message out and move on to the next project sooner than later.

I have no fear of failure. Many will enjoy this book, many won't get past the first chapter and many will think it's a ridiculous concept and never pick it up. That is OK! There are people who will be unlocked into their destiny and that is all that matters!

I'll share another failure with you. I value the advance of the Kingdom through church and house of prayer planting. I personally love the process of starting with nothing and watching God build a ministry that truly touches lives.

While leading Revival Church in the Detroit region, my family and I moved about thirty minutes north into a more rural area by the apple orchards. It is a different environment than where our church is, and I felt the birthing and planting bug start to buzz in me again. So, we planted Revival Church North in my living room.

We met for several weeks on Sunday mornings and drew a handful of interested people, but, I could sense early on that the necessary traction wasn't there. Just as quickly as I decided to plant the church, I punted. It was fourth down and we could go for it or we could admit failure and move on to the next project. If I was walking in pride, I would have fought to keep it going, but, rather, it was easy for me to let it go. That plant failed. So what? Clearly it wasn't meant to be, or the timing was off, and that's OK. Believe it or not, I lost literally zero emotional energy through that process. I woke up the next day and refocused, prayed more and talked to God about next steps. There was still much burning in me and there are missions to attend to.

Thomas Edison said, "None of my inventions came by accident. I see a worthwhile need to be met and I make trial after trial until it comes." (*Statement in a press Thomas Edison, Henry Ford, Harvey Firestone, Alexis Carrel & Charles Lindbergh (conference (1929), as quoted in Uncommon Friends: Life with 1987) by James D. Newton, p. 24*)

If there is a need that you are picking up on, get to work! Trial and error are both your friend! Don't allow an insecurity to keep you from being the one that God wants to use to bring transformation, whether it's in leading a Sunday School class, developing a Kingdom business, starting a church or doing anything else God is leading you to do!

Remember Gideon? All he knew was that he was the weakest and the least, yet all God called him was mighty man of valor! Gideon was cowardly, as was his entire community. They were in hiding from their enemy, afraid of losing their crops, their livelihood. They were experiencing failure after failure and their confidence was gone.

Judges 6:14-16 And the LORD turned to him and said, "Go in this might of yours and save Israel from the hand of Midian; do not I send you?" And he said to him, "Please,

Lord, how can I save Israel? Behold, my clan is the weakest in Manasseh, and I am the least in my father's house." And the LORD said to him, "But I will be with you, and you shall strike the Midianites as one man."

This is God's call to you! Don't fear opposition! Don't fear failure! God had ordered your steps you mighty man of valor! Don't wait for others to affirm you–you will be waiting for decades possibly! Don't wait for the perfect plan. Gideon advanced with one percent of the army available to him and told them to blow their trumpets and smash their jars. That doesn't sound like a good plan at all, but it was what God led them to do. God has a Gideon's army waiting for you to have the courage to respond immediately as an insignificant person with an insignificant plan and an insignificant army to lead them into their destiny! Those who perceive themselves to be insignificant are but a moment away from initiating a move of God that will be felt throughout the city!

Remember that failure is an event, not a person. -Zig Ziglar

Chapter Three
Pray Like Mad!

I know in the last chapter I said that you should not fear failure, and I meant it. But, I take it all back if you aren't a person who prays like mad. Today there are people running churches and ministries, and businesses and other endeavors for that matter, with barely a whisper of prayer.

A life of continual, fiery, passionate prayer is required for every Christian—and certainly for those who presume to have a calling to lead in ministry. Can you imagine where you will lead people if you aren't intimately connected to Jesus? Of course you can imagine it. People are doing it in churches all around the world. This is an indictment on Christians everywhere, and you are not going to add to the pandemic—you are going to lead, live and walk in the spirit as you pray continually!

It really is important that we hear God's voice, and it's not reserved for special, big decisions. This is the point! As we pray continually, it will be easy to make decisions on the fly! When you are a person of really intense and deep prayer, day and night, you will be in tune with the Lord non-stop. You can make quick decisions based on communication from God in real time!

It is extremely common for me to make decisions without "praying about it," and it can appear quite flippant. The truth is that I'm a walking house of prayer, and when I receive an impression from the Lord, it's easy for me to make a decision to act in that moment. In fact, when I combine a life of prayer with expected failures, making decisions and launching initiatives is a quick, constant process. I hear God, take a step, redirect and keep moving! I don't wait to receive all of the intelligence about my project on the front end because I'm confident that my life of prayer will keep the data coming at every step!

I could write on prayer here page after page as it's one of my key, life messages. However, it would be much more efficient to direct you to my book *Revelation Driven Prayer*. In that book I share remarkable stories of God moving in power as I made bold steps in the direction of his voice. You absolutely can, and should, hear God's voice and have confidence in what he is calling you to do.

Suffice it to say that you have literally no option but to pray—a lot. It's as non-negotiable as breathing. Prayer should mark your life as a fiery brand. Think about it this way: when you are not in a place of prayer, when you are not walking and living in the spirit, you are living in the natural. You are limited by natural wisdom and natural insight. It is simply not possible to fulfill supernatural mandates through natural methods.

When we pray, the supernatural is activated. In the supernatural place of the spirit, the prophetic jumps and kicks and it becomes quite easy and wildly adventurous to make life shifting decisions.

God had spoken to me several times in prayer to develop a unique, regional revival school and ministry here in Detroit. He revealed to me a model of another emerging and popular ministry that was very similar to what God has called me to birth.

Well, I let it simmer for a while, until one day in pre-service prayer at Revival Church God suddenly spoke. I am not a fan of using movie quotes in prophecy, but this was undeniable. God said, as I was pondering this mandate to launch a school of fire, "If you build it, they will come."

God must have watched Field of Dreams too. It was such a strong word, that I couldn't deny it. In fact, I didn't want to deny it. It was burning in me. I called everybody in the prayer room together and shared with them exactly what God had just said. We then prayed on it and after several moments, absolutely invigorated, we went into the church service.

Well after the service started, a certain man arrived, and at an appropriate moment during worship he asked if he could share a prophetic word. After giving him the green light, he stood up and simply said, "John, I don't know what this means specifically, but God wants you to know that if you build it, they will come." I was speechless.

We started theLab University in faith, even though we had no place to host it. We didn't have a building to meet in. In fact, God was very clear regarding obedience to this new mandate. He revealed that he wouldn't bring the increase if we used an excuse of not having a place to meet to cause a delay. If we didn't build it due to weak, human excuses, they would not come.

So, we started meeting at noon during the week at another ministry that allowed us access, and the rest is history. God moved, we found a property just before the first session began, and the people showed up to this new, unusual encounter driven school of fire. It is the most powerful ministry we are a part of to this day. Our students and team have been in over seventy Detroit area churches to host passionate prayer events, and this training in the fire has rocked countless hungry people.

As time went by, I met someone who had become a leader in the ministry that I was modeling theLab after. We were ministering in Colorado at a conference together, and I shared the story of how God called me to start theLab. When I got to the part where I said God used a cheesy movie quote to get my attention, "If you build it they will come," this leader was stunned and suddenly shouted, "Shut up!"

She was a bit freaked out! She asked if I had heard about the vision that God gave their leadership recently. I hadn't. There's no reason I would have. She said, "We were at a staff meeting and God spoke profoundly and urgently. He said, 'If you build it they will come.'" I got goose bumps!

She said that the leader immediately sent someone to get a DVD of Field of Dreams and they watched the movie for the rest of the staff meeting.

This is how prayer works! This is why you must pray and hear God and get lined up with what he is doing! He loves to confirm his word!

My advice is not for you to say prayers. It's to pray! Eliminate every distraction, every time-thief, every competing argument and pray! Pray in the Holy Spirit much more than praying with your understanding. Don't focus on petition, but rather on relationship. Get intimate with Jesus! Fall in love with him. Tell him about himself. Read the Bible and meditate on it. Enjoy Jesus!

Refuse to participate in anything that would hinder that relationship. Embrace holiness. Don't allow yourself to be entertained by anything on TV or in the movies or music that required the death of the one you are developing intimacy with. Be serious about your life and jealously guard the glorious, pure and overwhelming intimate relationship with the lover of your soul!

Until you are at a place of continually praying, you can't get too serious about ministry, but if you are with God continually, it is easy to launch and develop much!

Chapter Four
The Giant First Step

L et me attempt to set you free—the giant step of starting a new ministry or project is not really that big. I'm not saying it's not significant or important, or even a little overwhelming. I'm saying that you can get used to moving very quickly without all of the pieces of the puzzle fitting together.

I would rather launch today, and readjust ten times over the next year than over prepare for a year and launch then. I would have ten fewer life lessons and my personal growth would be delayed. Of course, the impact of the ministry would be minimized as well.

Now, please understand, I am not counseling you to move ahead of God. What I am doing is uncovering a misconception. Delay is not the default and safe way to handle decision making. Delay is as threatening to your mission as prematurely advancing. In fact, I'd go so far as to say that delay is more threatening than acting swiftly. If you act a little bit early, you can pull back and regroup. If you delay, you can miss the opportunity. Really, it's common sense. Would you rather show up an hour early or an hour late to a movie? If you arrive an hour late, you might as well not even enter the theater. But, if you arrive early, you can get some popcorn, listen to some music on your phone, play a game or even talk with the person you are going with! An early arrival ensures a more satisfying and complete experience.

The same is true with ministry projects. Unless God has given you the red light, start your engines!

One of my favorite quotes that has become a staple of theLab culture is this:

Early is on time, on time is late and late is unacceptable.

William Shakespeare said:

Better three hours too soon than a minute too late.

Again, remember, don't fear failure! Usually, the purpose for waiting is to minimize risk, but this delay is most often more risky than obedient advance. Many wait for the green light before moving when often the better plan is to keep moving until you see the red light!

Philippians 3:12-16 Not that I have already obtained this or am already perfect, but I press on to make it my own, because Christ Jesus has made me his own. Brothers, I do not consider that I have made it my own. But one thing I do: forgetting what lies behind and straining forward to what lies ahead, I press on toward the goal for the prize of the upward call of God in Christ Jesus. Let those of us who are mature think this way, and if in anything you think otherwise, God will reveal that also to you. Only let us hold true to what we have attained.

This passage reveals a principle that is valuable and scripturally sound—to understand there is always more to gain in God and it takes a short term memory of failures (and successes) and a fervent determination to press ahead! Paul says this is a mature way to live. Again, I want to make it perfectly clear—if the red light is on, don't move! But, as my three-year old daughter Ella shouts from the backseat when we are waiting at a traffic light, "Green light GO!" There's a time to press ahead, step on the gas and go, even if your GPS is only revealing the next turn to you.

Here's one example of many giant first steps: A couple friends from Kansas City were visiting us at our home in Detroit recently. We were casually discussing our ministries, our passion for advance and what God might be saying. We prayed fervently together and were just waiting for some direction. Then, suddenly, as two of us were sitting in my office, God downloaded an incomplete yet significant idea— launch theLab University online. It was an instant instruction and we instantly responded. Green light GO!

We called our other friend up and shared the vision and she was immediately on board. People have been asking us how they can experience our prayer movement and theLab from places outside of Detroit, and now we had the answer. Keep in mind, we had nothing more than a zing in our spirits and a big idea. So, what was our giant first step? It was easy. Secure a domain name, develop a website and assign teaching modules to each of us. All of that, including the website, was done within a matter of a few days!

It's very important to understand that vision, no matter how clear when you receive it, will fade if it isn't given proper attention. This is why instant action in some fashion is almost always mandatory. There was no red light, so delay was not the wise thing to do.

I designed the logo and the website. We decided on what each of us would be teaching. We discussed how to get the training videos created. We talked about marketing. We had buy in and we had commitment from all three of us. The action in those first few hours and days was critical! A giant first step, what some call rapid prototyping, is a very important part of the process.

Then, my friends went back to Kansas City, and we have had some communications and are waiting for some life situations to shift, so now, the project is temporarily on hold. Sometimes that happens. In fact, it often happens! We have to be prepared for redirects, shifts, unavoidable delays and major changes to the process. But, those must come after an initial giant step, not as we just wait around for some mythical perfect time to move.

There are a lot of people out there who have a misunderstanding of timing. They wait and wait for mostly undefined things to align, and then they wait some more, growing more frustrated by the minute.

I learned an amazing life lesson from my mom, unexpectedly, one day. I was recently married, and was living in Cleveland, Tennessee with my new wife, awaiting her graduation so we could move into full-time ministry. I knew that was God's will and I couldn't wait for it to happen!

Amy's college graduation date drew nearer, and there were no opportunities presenting themselves to us for ministry after she was finished with school. I was talking to my mom on the phone about the situation and she asked me a really unspiritual question, "So, have you submitted resumes?"

What? Now, Mom, that is not spiritual at all! (I thought it, but didn't say it!)

I was surprised that she offered such a natural, simple, obvious piece of advice. Where is the great wisdom that I was expecting? Well, it was right there in its simple glory.

After thinking about it, it made sense! After all, how would pastors who might be looking for a youth pastor even know I exist? Did I expect an angel to make an announcement to them in their church office? Would God write my name in the clouds above churches all over the world? I wish. That would be really cool! But, no, that is not to be expected.

So, I prayed and put together a fiery resume and sent it out all over the nation. The first response was from someone I had never heard of named Randy Clark. This was while he was pastoring a church in St. Louis and just after the Toronto Blessing had rocketed. Amy and I interviewed with him, and we also interviewed with a pastor in San Diego. After discovering Randy had narrowed down his search to two people, me being one of them, I had to let him know that I accepted the position in San Diego. I believe without question that I made the right choice, but I sometimes wonder what it would have been like to run with Randy Clark!

So, a non-step would have resulted in frustration, but, instead, my giant first step was a simple resume that resulted in quite an adven-

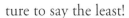

ture to say the least!

As I stated above, we have to be comfortable with redirects, shifts and even failed Plan A's that can lead us into Plan B or C. We have one life to live, and the time is limited. Again, I'd rather start many things and have success in one than start one thing, years down the road, and have success in it.

Jump!

The story of our move from the International House of Prayer in Kansas City to Detroit is a pretty remarkable one. There were several giant first steps involved in that process, and this story should help motivate you to jump!

We were in a very difficult season, having lost another baby to miscarriage (we have lost seven in total), and wondering what our next ministry step would be. We were done with our commitment at IHOPKC and I was yearning for the next assignment to show itself.

I met a man from Detroit at the coffee shop at IHOPKC who invited me, on the spot (God works that way sometimes!) to be the guest speaker at a week-long intensive at their house of prayer in the Detroit area. I felt it was God, so I agreed immediately. (That was an easy giant first step!)

The week I was in Detroit ministering was absolutely beyond human words. The man who led the ministry told me it was the closest to revival that he had ever been. People were literally encountering God in such a way that it left one young lady physically shaking for over 72 straight hours. Something had landed in Detroit!

We ended up developing a great relationship, and they flew me out five more times over the next several months to hold revival events. In the process, I felt God was clearly calling us to move from Kansas City to Detroit. Keep in mind, this was at a time when the nation was at the bottom of an economic collapse, and at a time when people were leaving Detroit by the multiplied thousands. Nobody, it seemed, was moving to Detroit.

My wife would admit that she was in the midst of the most trying time of her life. It was a true crisis of faith that she was valiantly working through, and, for her, moving into what felt more like a third-world mission assignment in Detroit was not what she wanted—not in the least.

But, she is faithfully devoted to Jesus, and she had become accustomed to giant first steps in our life. In fact, the move from Colorado Springs to Kansas City was nothing short of a stunning miracle (multiple miracles, in fact.) and she held out hope that our righteous steps toward Detroit or anywhere else would be ordered of the Lord.

We had recently bought a house in a suburb of Kansas City near the International House of Prayer called Grandview. Grandview is a nondescript, small residential town, yet it somehow ended up on Forbes Magazine's list of the fastest dying cities in America. Grandview was number eight. So, we lived in a dying city during the greatest national economic collapse in recent history, and we had to sell our house for full price (the only price that would enable us to pay it off).

My wife prayed. She actually put out a fleece. She told God that we would move to Detroit if he sold our house for full price within the next seven days. Otherwise, we'd move back to Colorado Springs to continue developing our ministry there, which is actually what she was pulling for!

We put the house on the market the next day, which was another immediate, giant step, and it did, in fact, sell for full price on the sixth day.

Thirty days later, we took another giant step by loading up the Penske truck and driving to Detroit—without any place to move our family or the tons of furniture and household items into. We parked the truck in a field, got into our car and started driving aimlessly around the Detroit region. On our second day of looking, God spoke to me and said, "The next house you see will be your home."

We ended up in Grosse Pointe, Michigan, which is a beautiful suburb on the lake just north of Detroit. We looked at a home there, offered $400 less per month for what they wanted for a lease, and they accepted. We literally moved in the next day! Amy loved her new home in her new city. I did as well.

While all of this was going on, we were also in discussions with the leader of the house of prayer in Detroit about launching a church out of that ministry. He and the team felt confirmed that it was at least something to explore, which we did. We were excited about taking the ministry to the next level and seeing what kind of strength might come by joining their and our efforts, passions and dreams. There was one issue, however, that had to be addressed. The leader of that house of prayer was also on staff of another church as an associate pastor. I had preached in that church myself, and the pastor there was excited about what God was doing.

Amy and I, before we left the Kansas City area, determined that we would not launch a church out of the house of prayer with our new ministry friend if the pastor of that church was not in agreement. We had a conference call with him, and he voiced disagreement. So, our attempted giant step of planting a church on the foundation of the house of prayer was stopped cold. Since we had already determined in our hearts to honor that pastor (which was important as we were entering new territory), it was a disappointment, but we understood that God was still very much in charge. On to Plan B.

When we arrived in Detroit, I started serving on the leadership team of the house of prayer, and shortly after we discussed plans to launch a ministry school there. It was something they had desired for a long time, and with the church plant nixed, this seemed like the perfect time to launch it. Everybody on the team was excited and on board. I was quick to help cast the vision and bring some organization to it. I knew in my spirit that Detroit needed a fiery ministry school, and, of course, this was well before God spoke to me about theLab. The school of fire was in my spirit, planted there by God.

I was ready to kick into a season of birthing, developing, re-directing, adjusting, succeeding and failing and ultimately equipping hungry, emerging firebrands in the new school of ministry. However, the leadership of the house of prayer started to feel out of step and, as the senior leaders of that ministry, they chose to put the breaks on the project. They, of course, had the right to do this, and I honored that decision. Again, I always try to stay emotionally prepared for surprises like this, so it wasn't too much of a disappointment. With the school plans ceasing, my role with that house of prayer lost definition, so I stepped off of the leadership team. However, I still rallied around their vision and enjoyed participating in their movement.

Of course, I still had a burning vision for revival in Detroit, and there was a reason God moved my entire family to this region that wasn't yet obvious. I awaited God's next signal. Launching a church out of the house of prayer that I initially connected with was not an option due to our agreement with the pastor that didn't feel like it was a good move. Developing a school within the house of prayer wouldn't come to pass either. We were now released to move into our own ministry, and a brand new adventure commenced!

Our next giant step was to announce a pre-launch meeting that would take place in our home—to discuss the possible planting of our second church. We had planted in Colorado, and were again ready to gather people together who could bring shocking impact to a region.

Just like before, we didn't have any extra money, and were not resourced any other way either. We just had a meeting. Do you feel called to start a church? Call a meeting, and a church just may be born! It could happen as early as next week! Pray, consider the timing, get the word out and meet! Yes, planting a church really is a piece of cake!

So, we met, and then met again the next week, and the next. The leader of the house of prayer joined our team of overseers, others were getting excited and Revival Church was born! People loved the vision, wanted to be a part of it, and started meeting and giving and praying and dreaming!

There were such amazing relationships between us and the house of prayer and the churches of the region—it felt great! A giant step was quite easy indeed!

But, soon after, our giant step into a terribly oppressed region would result in warfare. Like the Israelites crossing the Jordan into the Promised Land, we too took a giant step—into a land of giants.

The question is, will you function as a *Moses generation* who dies in the desert, or a *Joshua generation* who possesses the land?

Numbers 14:1-2 Then all the congregation raised a loud cry, and the people wept that night. And all the people of Israel grumbled against Moses and Aaron. The whole congregation said to them, "Would that we had died in the land of Egypt! Or would that we had died in this wilderness!

Joshua 3:17 Now the priests bearing the ark of the covenant of the LORD stood firmly on dry ground in the midst of the Jordan, and all Israel was passing over on dry ground until all the nation finished passing over the Jordan.

Chapter Five
A Land of Giants

We are called to take giant first steps—into a land of giants.

Numbers 13:25-33 At the end of forty days they returned from spying out the land. And they came to Moses and Aaron and to all the congregation of the people of Israel in the wilderness of Paran, at Kadesh. They brought back word to them and to all the congregation, and showed them the fruit of the land. And they told him, "We came to the land to which you sent us. It flows with milk and honey, and this is its fruit. However, the people who dwell in the land are strong, and the cities are fortified and very large. And besides, we saw the descendants of Anak there. The Amalekites dwell in the land of the Negeb. The Hittites, the Jebusites, and the Amorites dwell in the hill country. And the Canaanites dwell by the sea, and along the Jordan." But Caleb quieted the people before Moses and said, "Let us go up at once and occupy it, for we are well able to overcome it." Then the men who had gone up with him said, "We are not able to go up against the people, for they are stronger than we are." So they brought to the people of Israel a bad report of the land that they had spied out, saying, "The land, through which we have gone to spy it out, is a land that devours its inhabitants, and all the people that we saw in it are of great height. And there we saw the Nephilim (the sons of Anak, who come from the Nephilim), and we seemed to ourselves like grasshoppers, and so we seemed to them."

If you plan on taking new ground for the Kingdom, you better get used to giants. The report that the spies delivered was correct. There was good fruit to be had not to mention the milk and honey. It was as God had promised when he delivered them from Egypt! It would certainly be easy for them to see that God was in control, right?

You'll notice that the report also included a description of the giants in the land, the Nephilim that caused them to feel like grasshoppers in comparison. That was also a correct analysis.

You see, when God gives you an assignment, he will most always highlight the promise, the goal, the victory. He often chooses to leave out details like an army of giants that will attempt to kill you!

It is at this point where you will have to either lock in or turn and run. Are you one who is fearless and full of faith, ready to fight with the spirit of a victorious warrior, or are you troubled and timid? It's an important question. Be honest. The temptation right now, as you are sitting in a comfortable place reading this book is to boldly declare, "Bring it on! I'm a bold, fearless warrior!" But, then, what happens when someone begins to speak against you? How will you react when the giant spirit attempts to intimidate you with threat of loss and brokenness? Will you still stand? Are you willing to lose it all for the sake of God's calling on your life? You need to make that decision before you move out into battle.

1 Samuel 17:32 And David said to Saul, "Let no man's heart fail because of him. Your servant will go and fight with this Philistine."

Taking ground will always include giants. It doesn't matter

whether you are planting a church with the intention of impacting a neighborhood or starting a Kingdom business with designs to finance Kingdom work. The giants will resist you. No matter how exciting the planning stages are, be ready for the taunts and the threats and the arrows. The battle will come.

You might be wondering, "How in the world can dealing with evil, nasty, demonic giants be a piece of cake?"

It has to do with the condition of your heart! If you can live a life free of offense, with the ability to bless those who curse you, you will remain tender, joyful and full of faith! Yes, dealing with giants can be a piece of cake! David didn't even break a sweat!

> 1 Samuel 17:50-51 So David prevailed over the Philistine with a sling and with a stone, and struck the Philistine and killed him. There was no sword in the hand of David. Then David ran and stood over the Philistine and took his sword and drew it out of its sheath and killed him and cut off his head with it. When the Philistines saw that their champion was dead, they fled.

David was full of faith! He knew his God! He was not confused about the mission at all. While everybody else in the camp was waiting, delaying, wondering when the green light would shine, David didn't wait! He saw no red light. He didn't lean on human wisdom (by putting on Saul's armor). He refused every argument against advance. He ran without delay and did what should have been done long before—initiated freedom for his people.

When I started traveling to Detroit from Kansas City to minister, it felt like an open heaven! It sure seemed to be a giant-free zone! I wondered how anybody would ever want to leave Detroit—it felt like angels were breathing fire and God himself was taking up residence here!

As I shared previously, the first week I was here we experienced a legitimate move of God with the smell of revival all over it. People got suddenly hit by a glory train in shocking fashion. The word was spreading and hungry people kept showing up. Something significant was happening.

I was as surprised as everybody else, and I was humbled. I was also desperate for more, and quickly discovered that a lot of people in the Detroit region were as well. When I returned to Detroit month after month, I was welcomed into churches to minister. I was told that it was unprecedented for pastors in this region to open their pulpits like that—especially to someone they had never met! You see, I wasn't aware of the fierce spirit of competition between churches and ministries here. Every leader I met was warm and impressive!

I ministered to leadership teams, at weekend events and Sunday services, and time and again God moved. Finally, on my final trip to Detroit, I announced at a meeting at the house of prayer that my family and I were moving to Detroit to help in the pursuit of prayer-fueled revival. The place erupted in applause! I was excited and encouraged! God was on the move and revival was coming to Detroit!

When we finally did move and arrived on the scene with our moving truck, the feeling was electric. After we found our new home and announced that we were unloading the truck, people we didn't even know showed up to help. Our arrival was celebrated! We loved Detroit and Detroit loved us! What a rush!

Then the giants woke up.

As I share the rest of this story, it's important to understand that demons, not people, are the ones who are attempting to resist and destroy. I guarantee you and I have been unwitting tools in the hands of the enemy as he worked to shatter other people. I've met very good, wonderful people in this region, and some of them did in fact become resistant to our advance in ministry. It's freeing for me to understand that it's Satan who is resisting us, not people. It's extremely easy for me to smile wide when I see friends who have troubled us in the past. You must get to this place as well. Be unoffendable so you can serve and love those who resist you. Forgive them, they know not what they do!

1 Peter 5:6-9 Humble yourselves, therefore, under the mighty hand of God so that at the proper time he may exalt you, casting all your anxieties on him, because he cares for

you. Be sober-minded; be watchful. Your adversary the devil prowls around like a roaring lion, seeking someone to devour. Resist him, firm in your faith, knowing that the same kinds of suffering are being experienced by your brotherhood throughout the world.

As the above passage reveals, in the face of giants and threats of attack, our strategy begins and ends with humility. The giants will absolutely show up, and you will lose the battle they initiate if you are not humble. Additionally, we trust God, remain sober and watch. Why do we watch? We will come to a point of required response, in one way or another, when your adversary causes suffering through an attempt to devour you.

If your assignment has eternal worth, it will absolutely be attacked simply because it is a threat to the kingdom of darkness. The giants will arise, the lions will prowl and many attempts will be made to distract, discourage and destroy you and your ministry. And, sadly, many of the attempts will come as a result of friendly fire—through people we deeply love and honor—fellow brothers and sisters.

This point will either validate or disqualify you so pay attention! When good people do evil things to you, how will you react? The way you hold your heart matters! The bigger the vision, the more threatening you will be to the status quo that is affirmed by the majority of the Christian community.

So, again, we don't wrestle against people, against flesh and blood, but what can happen is that the enemy can get tricky and meddle in the emotions of amazing people, who as a result, can either intentionally or unwittingly facilitate opposition against you. If you understand this truth, it will actually be extremely easy to love and bless those people with little emotional energy wasted in the midst of the conflict. You will legitimately celebrate these people while you assault with violence the enemy that is attempting to manifest and operate through them.

The reason why we have to talk about this instead of avoiding a sensitive issue is simply to follow 1 Peter 5 protocol. We must be watchful. We must know what the enemy's schemes are.

As I explained previously, the initial ministry projects that we gave ourselves to didn't pan out. The proposed church plant within the house of prayer couldn't develop out of respect of the pastor who didn't support it. The proposed school in the house of prayer was called off as well. After those decisions, I honored their authority and was excited to serve along side them any way I could. They are special people and I'm sure we'll keep ministering together in the years ahead.

What I didn't realize was, sadly, the initial celebration of the mission for revival had faded for some people in the region. My heart was consumed with the mission of revival in Detroit, yet support for that pursuit was not as exuberant as before—though many others were picking up the fire and running hard with us. That's typical of ministry. People you think will be running with you may not choose to do so, and others may surprise you with their passion for revival!

Resistance is to be expected. After we started Revival Church, the enemy unleashed his hordes! The giants in the land were alert and they didn't play fair. The enemy resisted our new church vehemently! That resistance would have stopped us if it made me bitter. I would have been disqualified from my mission due to a failure of my heart. Instead, my wife and I checked our hearts repeatedly to double and triple check and make sure we were loving and serving well and hadn't failed to honor others in any way. (One of the quickest ways to grow is by listening to the voice of your critics!)

I realized that regardless of the level of support (or lack of it) I received, the mission remained. So, what did we do when resistance increased? We used it as a catalyst to connect with pastors and leaders all over Detroit who have revival burning in their hearts!

Since those early days just a few years ago, my team and I have been in at least seventy different churches to hold fiery, unifying prayer events! Over seventy pastors in the Detroit region embraced us with open arms and we have been so blessed to serve them! We pray that their ministries explode! If I had handled my heart wrongly early on, those doors would never have opened and we would be struggling, disgruntled and confused as favor faded away.

We have watched God work wonders through key revival events here, and we have truly barely begun. The giants are still here, and they are not happy about revival. If we keep our hearts healthy and continue to bless and celebrate other people, stay friendly with our critics and love deeply, we will be part of something that I truly believe can be history making.

So, yes, it is a piece of cake to deal with giants, even when wounding comes. It's a piece of cake to remain childlike, to refuse offense and to smile widely as you honor others and keep moving forward as servants of the King!

Chapter Six
Can You See It?

Starting a ministry really is a piece of cake—as long as you can see it and taste it before you eat it. You must have vision.

I can't overestimate the importance of burning with a mandate that you can see, smell, taste and feel before you take your first step toward fulfilling it.

There are entire books written on this topic, so I won't take much time here, but it is extremely important to truly possess vision before you move forward. Before you get too stressed out, having vision does not mean you know how to fulfill it! You simply have to see it.

I often share a couple of diagrams when coaching on vision. If you are familiar with sailing, you understand what tacking is. When attempting to move into resistance (the wind), you will never sail directly toward your goal. You will move at an angle left and right. It's important to get comfortable with this type of movement—it may look like you aren't moving toward your goal, but in reality you are.

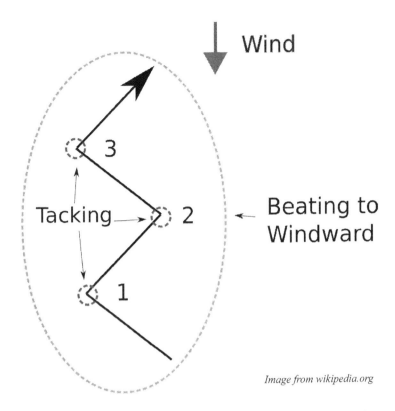

Image from wikipedia.org

Another way to consider vision is this: visionaries will see the far off mountain peak as the goal, but will rarely see the valleys, drop-offs, wild animals and other unknowns that lurk between. These unknowns are not reason enough to delay the journey. The vision, if it burns in you, will take you through!

Vision that is birthed by God is mind-blowingly potent. I mean that in the most literal sense. When vision is birthed, it is alive and active. Here's another short story to help you understand.

In the late 1990's I was the youth pastor of a very successful, fast growing church in the north suburbs of Dallas. The church building was new and situated on a busy street in a well-to-do area. There were around 1,200 people who attended, and they were beginning to run out of space to host them all.

They also had a large plot of land that was undeveloped next to their main property, and it was on that empty ground that I saw it.

God dropped a vision for a new youth center that would be unlike anything else in the nation—a place that any young person would crave to hang out in. I didn't have all of the details, but I had the vision—a region shaking ministry center where hundreds of teens could encounter the fire of God.

I knew there were "wild animals and drop-offs" between where I was and the fulfillment of the vision, but do you think that stopped me? Was my zeal tempered? No way.

I shared the vision with my pastor, who did not appear whatsoever to be on the same page as me. I left that meeting feeling extremely underwhelmed with his response. He encouraged me to share the vision with one of the financial trustees, mostly, it seemed, to let me down softly without totally discouraging me.

I did meet with the trustee, who himself was extremely wealthy in addition to acting as a steward for this heavily resourced church, with the hope that he would catch the vision. I wanted him to see what I saw. I don't know that he ever did. His response seemed a bit ridiculous if not condescending, though I don't believe that was his intent.

In fact, he was acting as a true king in the Kingdom. He challenged me. He knew that true vision would have to be acted on even before the resource was there. In hindsight, he was not condescending, he was calling me to invest in the process.

What was his instruction? He offered to match dollar for dollar up to a certain amount (I forgot what the amount was, but $40,000 rings a bell) anything that I was able to raise toward the development of this youth center. The reason I left that meeting deflated was because I knew the vision had at least a $5 million dollar price tag on it. The vision seemed to die before it began, and I never discussed it with the pastor or any other decision makers in the church again.

I ended up moving on from that church to plant Revolution Church in Colorado. Several years later, I heard something that still results in my spirit burning.

The pastor of that church had just completed a major fundraising campaign to gather finances for an expansion of their maxed out sanctuary. People had bought into that vision and gave extravagantly, and everything was a go for the construction to begin.

One Sunday morning, the pastor was driving to church, and in very unusual fashion for him, a strong prophetic word landed in his spirit regarding a major and sudden change of direction. God made it clear that he was not to expand the sanctuary with the funds that had been raised, but that he was to use the money to build the most impacting youth center in the nation.

He was unsure about how people would receive this news, since they so graciously gave toward another vision. Their gifts were earmarked. That morning, in front of 1,200 people including trustees, staff and other leaders, he revealed what God surprised him with in the car on the way to the church that morning.

I was told that he received a standing ovation. That vision that I played a very small part in was now fulfilled—they did in fact build a $5 million youth center on that empty plot of ground. I saw it, cast the vision, and it is there today—though I've never seen it with my eyes even to this day.

You can head over to Google and search for 2435 Hebron Parkway, Carrollton, Texas. Check out the street view on the map and you'll see the church to the left, and the youth center on the right—sitting on what used to be empty ground.

Stay The Course

As you launch out, you must have vision, or you will not stay the course. You can't keep moving toward a goal that is constantly changing or is unclear. If you as a leader are shaky in this area, it will be extremely easy to compromise as external pressures and alternative insights present themselves.

Will you advance toward your vision, or will you allow it to shift like a weathervane, whichever way the wind may blow?

James 1:5-8 If any of you lacks wisdom, let him ask God, who gives generously to all without reproach, and it will be given him. But let him ask in faith, with no doubting, for the one who doubts is like a wave of the sea that is driven and tossed by the wind. For that person must not suppose that he will receive anything from the Lord; he is a double-minded man, unstable in all his ways.

Keep in mind, your temporary direction will constantly change, as you tack or move through the valleys toward the mountain peak, but your eyes must remain fixed on the goal.

God will give you wisdom and revelation, and your job is to believe what he says! Don't conform the vision to external demands!

The temptation is often to transform the culture to match the people instead of transforming people within the culture and vision God has called you to establish. If you stick to your vision, you'll lose some people, but if you conform to the people you'll lose some vision. When that happens, you'll lose people anyway.

Proverbs 29:18 Where there is no prophetic vision the people cast off restraint, but blessed is he who keeps the law.

People will scatter. They will break away.

It breaks my heart and causes my head to spin when I hear of leaders who don't have vision, or, even worse, they have adopted someone else's. For example, how often have you heard the following vision statement?

To know God and make him known

That's great, but that's not vision. It's certainly not personal. And it's clearly not specific.

Vision comes directly from God to you. You'll receive it through fervent prayer, and it will absolutely possess you!

When we moved to Manitou Springs, Colorado to launch the church there, my vision was so overwhelming and personal that it captured not only my attention, but my emotion and radical commitment to see it come to pass. I saw an entire region transformed by the fire of God, and I had insights on what that would look like. I had visions and encounters that were undeniable.

I'll never forget a life-altering moment at a restaurant in Colorado Springs shortly after we moved to the region and started the church. I met a man who had some history as a key intercessor in the region. It was an honor to eat lunch with him and to hear his heart for ministry in the Pikes Peak area. He very casually asked me, "So, what's one thing you are craving for God to do as you start on your mission here?"

That was an easy question and I had an immediate answer! You see, we started the church with nothing—no money, no backing, no resources and no people. As a young church planter and a first time senior leader, I felt very much alone and vulnerable.

I answered his question, "I want God to send someone to me who has the same vision as me to run with me."

He said, "It will never happen."

Great. That was just the encouragement I needed!

He continued by saying, "Vision is personal. God gave it personally to you, and there is not a single person in the world other than you who has the vision. You have the assignment and the responsibility to fulfill it."

He went on to explain that God will certainly send people to me to support my vision and to help strengthen it, but, at the end of the day, the vision was mine and I had to communicate it and do whatever was necessary to see it come to pass.

That liberated me! I stopped waiting for affirmation or further confirmation. It was time to get to work! God gave me a job and I was on the clock.

Chapter Seven
Are You Covered?

Just as I was about to start writing this chapter, I received a Facebook comment from someone who said, "I'm led by the Spirit and I follow no man."

I nicely challenged her by explaining that her position is unbiblical. There are millions of people who are angry at and afraid of leadership, and there are resulting theologies that have been invented that are contrary to what we see in the Bible. Wounded people tend to feel safer and freer when not submitted and connected to authorities, but the contrary is actually true. God has designed spiritual authority to protect us, to sharpen us and to equip us.

I wrote my book *Covens in the Church* on this topic, and I'd encourage you to read it if you struggle with rejection or mistreatment from spiritual leaders. You won't be able to move out in healthy leadership if you don't deal with that first.

Romans 13:1-3 Let every person be subject to the governing authorities. For there is no authority except from God, and those that exist have been instituted by God. Therefore whoever resists the authorities resists what God has appointed, and those who resist will incur judgment. For rulers are not a terror to good conduct, but to bad. Would you have no fear of the one who is in authority? Then do what is good, and you will receive his approval…

If we want to live unafraid of authority, we simply do what is good. Honor authority and refuse to resist them.

When starting into ministry, it's a wonderfully healthy and necessary step to align yourself with mature leaders who will speak into your life and protect you in times of crisis. Having a spiritual covering is something that is extremely desirable! I can't imagine ever ministering outside of it.

When we were in the process of starting Revival Church in the Detroit area, the first practical step I took was to secure a covering. You'll remember that we submitted to the authority of a local pastor within the agreed boundaries of the house of prayer where we initially started ministering. Once we were released from leadership there, that alignment ended and it was critical for us to find more permanent alignment with a regional, spiritual and governmental authority. As a regional ministry, our covering had to cover that geography at least.

I knew from the moment we arrived, in my spirit, that we were to align with particular network that was led by a apostolic leader with key regional authority. After connecting with that ministry, I continued in prayer regarding this important decision.

We were actually pursued by three other ministry networks as word got out that we were starting the church. I knew we had to make the right decision, and none of those options felt right. One of the network leaders, whom I knew and had ministered for in his church in the area, was quite determined to have me join his denomination. However, I just couldn't get comfortable with that idea. It wasn't God's will for us.

That leader ended up leaving the denomination. Sometimes hindsight and foresight are one in the same. I just never felt that decision would work out well for me if I chose to join with them. I was right.

So, of course, we did in fact join with our preferred network, and I can't begin to explain the blessing it has been to us.

Earlier this year our church was suddenly struck with a challenge as we lost some key leadership. My wife and I and our core team were hit pretty hard as a handful of friends in our church separated out suddenly. I've never been more surprised by anything in all my 23 years of ministry, and we had to immediately kick into crisis management.

My first step was to contact the network's lead associate, and submit to her leadership and covering as we worked through this challenge. Without exaggeration, I have never been more impressed with someone in ministry before! They dove into this situation that was extremely distracting for us, and stood with us from beginning to end.

Without their covering, prophetic insight, wisdom and their apostolic, governmental authority in the region, the outcome could have been much more difficult. In fact, God used the crisis to rally together those who were burning with our vision, and unity is at an all-time high! We continue to pray blessing for those who left and are free and alive as we continue on our journey of revival in Detroit! Right alignment is critical!

I also have others who I seek counsel from. It takes humility to admit that you need other people to draw wisdom and protection from. If you are thinking of moving out without apostolic covering, you are setting yourself and others up for disaster.

It's true that submitting to authority and aligning with them does result in restrictions and boundaries, but we should appreciate them and not resist them. Biblical boundaries as expressed through covenant relationships are life-giving and help in your own maturing process.

It is nonsensical to presume we are always making right choices, and by submitting ourselves to others we can stay accountable and in a position of humility. If we remain teachable, our covering can really pour into us, refine us and call us higher! They will support the mission God has called us to.

Chapter Eight
Momentum & Resources

A lot of energy is given to the generation of resources and momentum. Resources are needed to build the machine and momentum is important to make progress.

First, I want to affirm that investing time, energy, prayer and passion into both resource and momentum development is fully appropriate. Give yourself to marketing, casting vision and creating motion for your project.

Second, don't compromise. Your goal isn't to gather resources and to maintain momentum. Your goal is, well, your goal. The journey toward that goal, when compromise is not an option, will most usually result in seasons of struggle, loss, backpedaling and lack of motion. Whatever you do, don't change your message or your mandate to gain buy in! Prepare for resistance and rejection–and celebrate when you maintain your standard and when those who are assigned by God to partner with you show up for work.

There will always be extreme pressure to adjust your vision, sometimes ever so slightly, to be more appealing to others, but it's this adjustment that will put your entire mission at jeopardy.

I'll just say it—when God gives you your mandate, you must be both humble and stubborn—and no matter how humble you are, your stubborn disposition will invite trouble. Convincing arguments from wonderful people can lead you to compromise. Don't do it. Love people in your stubborn, unmoving determination to obey God. In ministry, there are negotiables and non-negotiables. Never move on the non-negotiable vision God has called you to steward.

Mission Confusion

One of the most difficult barriers to overcome when developing a ministry according to a fresh but unfamiliar vision is the *supposed to's*. There can be confusion on the purpose and process of the mission.

In our Western church culture, there are numerous focuses, ministries, attitudes and functions that are just "supposed to" be a significant part of the ministry. When attention isn't given to what others presume are non-negotiable, discord and accusation can quickly enter the camp. Many leaders (most) will diplomatically, democratically attempt to avoid discord by entertaining these arguments in the name of unity. However, the result is false-unity around the desires of people instead of true unity around the mandates of God. How can you tell the difference? False unity is inclusive of all, true unity requires agreement that most are unwilling to adhere to.

Under Moses, there was unspoken accusation that he was more interested in his vision to enter the Promised Land, and that he wasn't concerned for his people and their safety. Their arguments were convincing—and they actually won the argument—and then died in the desert.

We recently went through a trying season at Revival Church that highlights this point very well.

Our mandate has always been unique. As a ministry of reformation, it is *by design* initiating disruption and recalibration, and this will always cause trouble. I won't go into the details, but suffice it to say that God gave me a very clear prophetic word when I was leading a ministry in Colorado to transition from ministering to people to ministering to God. I was to vertically focus on God and draw others into that encounter with me. That vision is quite offensive as it takes the primary focus off of people and puts it on God.

As a result, Revival Church would not look like a typical church and would not focus on many of the expected ministries that you find in other churches. When we went through our trying time, there were some amazing friends who were wired a bit differently, and who were seeking some ministry focuses that were good, but not what we were to facilitate at Revival Church. There was confusion in the camp as I was running one way and they wanted to run in a slightly different direction.

It was presumed that our church, or any church, is "supposed to" be pastor led with a focus on community. Revival Church is Apostle led with a focus on intercession. Mostly vertical with a little horizontal. Our friends saw a lack of focus on community, and the lack of pastoral ministry, as a problem while we saw it as intentional and core to our mission. We are a prayer-centric equipping center as opposed to a community-centric family style church. The family church is the expected norm today, and it does truly take quite an effort of vision casting to break through that expectation.

To see reformation, you will have to work hard to cast the vision, and then to stay true to it. Our culture of fiery intercession and equipping awakeners has resulted in a surprising and deep community of people that love one another and who are keeping their gaze upon the Lord together! We have burning ones who pray as their primary ministry, and enjoy doing it with friends and family around them.

At the International House of Prayer in Kansas City, you don't see a lot of hanging out for the sake of hanging out, but you did see people in the prayer room together ministering to the Lord. That culture is a problem for those who don't crave to pray, but can you imagine IHOPKC bending to develop a culture that doesn't emphasize prayer? It's nonsensical. But, it's only nonsensical now because they have gone through much trial and trouble to set their culture. They stayed true to the mandate even when it was confusing to more traditional Christians.

At Revival Church our plan is to go through the same process to set a similar culture. What does this have to do with resources and momentum? A lot.

A counter-culture movement loses the resources of the many, and the lack of many supporters and partners results in momentum slowing to a crawl. We had to decide between money and movement in the short term and stubbornly sticking to our core values. No matter what you are attempting to develop, you will also have to make this choice over and over again.

I once heard a story about a small church that had some great momentum and sufficient resources. One of their primary financial givers approached the young pastor and said he was ready to make a significant donation. The only catch was that he felt it would be best for the culture they are trying to develop at the church to encourage an *undesirable* , unkempt lady to move on to another church. The young pastor refused, the financial giver left the church and the undesirable lady remained. She was actually very much a part of the culture and vision of the church, and she was desired more than the manipulative person with money in his hands.

That church grew to over 14,000 people and that lady became the matriarch of the church. She held a seat of honor on the front row until she passed away many years later.

Resources and momentum temporarily slowed while the right thing was done.

When you adhere to God's risky vision, you are at great risk of losing the resources of the majority. Since an apostolic spirit of reformation is initiating change to the status quo, the high majority of those who still value the status quo will not invest in your vision.

The cash flow of your church or ministry is absolutely at risk of slowing to a crawl. Are you OK with that? Pastors may have to surrender their security and salaries, get secular jobs and trust that God will truly provide—because many people will stop giving.

They will also not show up. They won't run with you. Are you OK with that or will you look for a happy medium that's appealing to the majority?

If you pray for a remnant, don't be surprised when a remnant shows up—and the majority leaves. At Revival Church, I really do want hundreds to show up each week. We are looking for 1000 fiery intercessors to pray for Detroit. But, I am willing to sacrifice their investment for the sake of staying true to our mission.

I have a lot of weaknesses. That's not false-humility, it's true. Just ask my wife! However, I am convinced that I am skilled just enough to grow a church, with the right team, to possibly 250. We had a church consultant years ago that said we had what it took to grow a church to 300-400.

Why and I revealing this? To let you know how easy it might be to sacrifice the mission for the sake of personal satisfaction.

A church of 250 would ensure that I would have a great salary and the ability to pay other key staff members. We would also have significant resources to grow and facilitate additional ministries. We'd have the people and the money to do much. It would feel great to be *successful* in the eyes of man.

In our recent trial, some friends were focused on church growth and on creating a vibrant, exciting atmosphere with people who were deeply connected to one another. This sounds great! And, I actually want this too. However, this is very important—that goal is not the goal. It is actually more of a desire than a strategic focus.

Yes, a lot of people gathering together each week can be very good, but I had already made the decision that we would not compromise the vision for the sake of resources—be it money or people or an energetic environment. I'm willing to run with a remnant and keep investing time and energy in my graphic and web design business to help pay the bills.

The resources Revival Church needs are burning, interceding prayer warriors who minister to God night and day. Any compromise of the vision would ensure those people won't show up. I've counted the cost, and that is my goal, no matter how great the challenge or how injurious it is to my ego, energy, time or ability to grow. In fact, the opportunity for humility and challenge is very good for me.

We made another vision-driven decision at Revival Church that directly impacts our resources. God was firm—do not seek after a worship leader or a worship team. You can be fairly certain that you won't grow beyond a small group without a worship leader. Amy and I have had a few amazing worship leaders over the past 22+ years of ministry, yet it has been difficult to find those who are radically, wildly invested in a lifestyle of fervent, never-ending prayer. We are going to use IHOPKC and other worship sessions on video until God leads musicians to us who pray night and day.

My wife and I were talking last night about this. Maybe this strategy could in fact work in a reformed church model. Maybe there will be churches of several thousand who don't have an in house worship team and instead, using media, worship together as remote, prayer invested worship teams lead the way. I can see it working. But, in the mean time, I'm convinced our numbers will remain small and our resources limited with this strategy—and I'm absolutely OK with that.

Small numbers and minimal buy-in are extremely hard for many people to look past. Staying the course on the way to mission fulfillment will result in that small remnant running with you, and for some, small numbers look like failure. The momentum won't be there. That in itself can result in lost hope. This is not good! This is why unity around the vision is so critical. You must have buy in from those who are running with you.

Again, the vision is NOT a large group of people. It's a fulfilled mission! I have to communicate this so false-expectations don't result in frustration.

Recently our worship team moved on, and this is when we decided to hold off on finding a new one. I knew numbers would drop, and they did. I also knew that I had a job ahead of me of communicating the true vision. Our vision is not to add people, and I had to make that clear. Anybody, including myself, loves a big crowd. There's some sense of accomplishment when that happens. Momentum is addictive. However, it really is not the goal. I have led ministries that had decent sized crowds, and a sense of momentum, but I was grieved. We were growing with people who didn't fully buy into the mission.

Trust me, I'd rather function without visible momentum while running with a few who are all in than with a crowd of people who are mostly there because of the experience. This is a huge point!

That being said, I am looking forward to the day when many

buy into the vision and we actually see stadiums filled with burning intercessors! Now, that's momentum! But, I don't want to see a stadium filled with people who are only there for the experience. I'd rather buy a ticket to an NFL game at packed stadium and be legitimately entertained than attempt to spiritualize an electric quasi-worship-fest with an arena full of interested but non-invested people.

If we want momentum, we can create momentum. Just gather people around a self-satisfying, entertaining message and slap the name of Jesus on it. Or, you can reveal the costly, deadly message of the cross and call people to a life of inconvenient intercession and spend years and decades creating a prayer movement. I choose the latter.

Of course, I'm sharing about my personal ministry journey, but this principle must be applied to any endeavor, whether secular or ministry, either small or large. Seek after resources and momentum as they are important, but don't ever lose sight of the goal. Expect challenge and remain humble and watch God move—maybe not immediately, but eventually.

Don't forget that Joseph had a critical vision for his life, and he could have compromised at any point to avoid the pit or the prison. He did not and his family and his people were saved.

Chapter Nine
Marketing Your Ministry

As a web and graphic designer I interact quite a bit with pastors and others who are looking to get their message out there. I also run into Christians who are nervous about the concept of marketing. For them it has a very secular, humanistic feel to it. I do understand wrestling with this as it's right to ensure our motives are pure.

That being said, I actually believe we have a responsibility to market, at least in measure. Why? I'll answer that question with a question. Do you believe there are people that you don't yet know who can experience Jesus through your new ministry venture? Then you need to communicate that as effectively as you can! It's not complicated—the more people that come in contact with your ministry, the more that can be transformed by Jesus.

I've heard Christians say something like, "If your ministry is burning in revival, you won't need to market!" Let's presume I agree with this statement (I don't). Is your ministry burning in revival now? No? Well, then you need to get your message out there so the necessary people can learn about the opportunity to contend toward revival together! Marketing helps draw in the people and resources you need to fulfill your mission.

Preaching is marketing. Sending emails about your ministry is marketing. Talking to friends about it is marketing. Handing out business cards is marketing. Marketing is simply intentional communication about what you believe to be a life-changing message and ministry. When people hear about it, the opportunity for Jesus to impact them is presented.

So, it makes sense to communicate with excellence, in such a way that people are convinced of your credibility. Clear, professional marketing reveals that you are serious about what you are initiating. Sloppy, amateurish design and execution reveals that you also approach other parts of your life and ministry the same way—and more than not people will avoid association with you. It's a difficult truth, but a truth nonetheless.

Can you imagine McDonalds or Starbucks or any number of other successful secular companies refusing to invest time, energy and finances into effective marketing? What if they just found some teenager that dabbles in web design and have them take over the marketing responsibilities and website design project? It doesn't make sense for them, and it doesn't for you either!

When I was on staff at the International House of Prayer, I served initially on the graphic design team. It was an incredibly impressive operation! There were clear standards that were communicated in a well thought out style guide. These standards ensured the marketing message of the ministry remained consistent throughout every department and that it didn't result in confusion. On the contrary, their role was to ensure that the mission of the ministry was extremely easy to understand and that any potential for confusion regarding that mission was dealt with before it could manifest.

This worldwide ministry exists in a storefront in an unimpressive section of southern Kansas City, Missouri. On my first trip to IHOPKC, I was shocked at what I saw. Their marketing was so professional and excellent that I presumed their physical location would look more like a modern arena than like a simple storefront next to a liquor store on a lazy residential street.

Someone once told me that I had a Gideon anointing in regard to marketing. I'm not sure if it was a complement or a slam, but I'll take it as a compliment! My marketing was so excellent and consistent that people presumed I was a much larger ministry than I was. Now, that was not because I was misrepresenting my ministry, but because I had adopted some of the same proven marketing principles that every successful organization does.

So, since this book is titled Piece of Cake, this must mean that marketing is simple and easy as well, right? Yes!

When starting a ministry or a project, here's what I do:

- **I setup my website immediately.** Some people presume this to be a very involved step. It is not! At times I'll work with clients who overcomplicate the web design process. To them, multiple meetings are required to discuss the numerous facets of the design process. They see it as being a multi-month project. It should not be!

  In my business, people can have a simple website that's absolutely stunning, functional and easy to manage ready to go in three business days! This is a custom designed site that costs next to nothing! All you have to do is get your domain name, find a design professional, submit your order and let them do the work!

  Whatever you do, don't be tempted to find an amateur to do the design! I've designed some beautiful websites only to have the client add graphics and make other changes themselves—which most usually disqualifies their site from a chance at being in my portfolio! In fact, I bet only 25% of the sites I design are portfolio worthy for this very reason. Don't turn pretty into ugly by putting your hands where only the professionals should touch!

- **I become very active on social media.** When I say active, I mean very active. This is the best free marketing you can find, but you have to invest in it by posting and engaging in conversations many times a day. You can use a third party tool like Hootsuite or Sprout Social to post to multiple sites at once, schedule posts and interact with people. Statistics reveal that updates to your various web based accounts such as Facebook, Twitter, your website and blog must total more than twelve per day—at a minimum! For me, I'll post an Instagram video, followed by an interesting quote on Facebook and Twitter, and then, later on a Youtube video where I discuss what's burning on my spirit that day. I'll write articles and post them to my website's blog and also respond to the conversations that it initiates. Again, twelve updates per day is the absolute minimum if you want people to be impacted by your message to the degree they should be!

- **I send emails to my subscribers multiple times a week.** Email is king. That has not changed, even in a world dominated by Facebook and Twitter. Get your message into people's inboxes regularly, and be sure there is a call to action! Where do you want your relationship with them to go? Is there a meeting you are inviting them to? Have them RSVP. Are you directing them to visit your website? Make it clear. Is there a product you are selling? Make it easy for them to purchase it. Just like your website, and all other marketing for that matter, ensure your email blast is professional and that the design communicates that.

- **I consider using paid ads.** When it makes financial sense, I will use Google and Facebook ads to get our ministry in front of more people. You can set a budget and choose to, for example, spend $10 a day on the low end or much more on the high end. Google tends to work best for those who are intentionally looking for a church (for example) while Facebook is great for alerting people of something they might be interested in, but wasn't necessarily looking for, like a special conference or to promote a new resource.

- **I produce some limited printed materials.** Printing is so cheap these days that it's an easy decision to print a few thousand club cards or even simple business cards that can be passed out. Again, the design has to be awe inspiring!

And, there you have it! It really is that easy to get your message out to the ones God is desiring to connect to your ministry. And, by all means, be instant in your approach! I often have domains secured, sites developed and materials ready before the ministry has even launched. By this time next week, you could have a Facebook page, a Twitter account, a new, professional designed website, a growing email marketing list and a few thousand printed cards ready to go! (But, you have to start working today!)

Chapter Ten
What About Money & Legalities?

Disclaimer: This book is intended to encourage you to develop your ministry, and is not intended to be a source for legal advice regarding non-profits, ministries or other endeavors. You are encouraged to do your homework and discover what your legal responsibilities include.

Never, ever, ever allow lack of money or red tape to keep you from taking the first step. Why? You may wait years to start while people's lives are hanging in the balance.

Amy and I have never had extra money when we launched a church or ministry endeavor. We just did it. We didn't wait.

I'll talk more about the need for urgency in a later chapter, so with that being said, what should be considered regarding finances and legalities?

First, you will have to be comfortable being bold in your requests to invest financially into your ministry. There is no room for false-humility here! Is your project worthy of investing into? If not, I doubt your project was initiated by God. If so, honor people by casting the vision and giving them the joyous opportunity to financially support it!

Of course, you must realize that it is God who brings the increase, but, he does so through people. So, you don't rely on people, but you do call people to respond to what the Holy Spirit is speaking to them. There are two directions that people need communication from—God, who reveals to them the opportunity to give, and the one that is called to steward their financial gift.

So, God may be putting it on someone's heart to give, but they may not have clarity on where or how to give (we see in part). We then can cast the vision, and that vision might trigger in them the call of God to respond. To make it plain, you have to ask for money.

Paul was quite bold when dealing with finances, but we also see that he remained humble while he communicated the biblical principle:

> 1 Corinthians 9:9-14 For it is written in the Law of Moses, "You shall not muzzle an ox when it treads out the grain." Is it for oxen that God is concerned? Does he not certainly speak for our sake? It was written for our sake, because the plowman should plow in hope and the thresher thresh in hope of sharing in the crop. If we have sown spiritual things among you, is it too much if we reap material things from you? If others share this rightful claim on you, do not we even more? Nevertheless, we have not made use of this right, but we endure anything rather than put an obstacle in the way of the gospel of Christ. Do you not know that those who are employed in the temple service get their food from the temple, and those who serve at the altar share in the sacrificial offerings? In the same way, the Lord commanded that those who proclaim the gospel should get their living by the gospel.

I love verse eleven. It reveals Paul's boldness and his determination to have his mission resourced. God gave him a responsibility to get the job done, and he knew that participation from others was required for it to happen. Again, it's God's design—he facilitates finances through people for the sake of Kingdom advance.

False-humility can keep us under-resourced, and that has impact on the mission.

When I was leading the ministry in Colorado, we went through quite a financial crisis. Due to an important shift in the focus of the ministry, we knew that some key givers would probably be moving on, and this did in fact happen.

There was a man named Russ who was born to give extravagantly. He was a king in the Kingdom. In the midst of this crisis, I had to start looking for a part-time job as my salary in the church was cut in half. Russ just couldn't see how this was good for the ministry, and he came to me one day to discuss it. Russ had always given quite significantly and was already a blessing. He told me that he knew my job was to be in the place of prayer. He was affirming Acts 6:2-4:

> Acts 6:2-4 And the twelve summoned the full number of the disciples and said, "It is not right that we should give up preaching the word of God to serve tables. Therefore, brothers, pick out from among you seven men of good repute, full of the Spirit and of wisdom, whom we will appoint to this duty. But we will devote ourselves to prayer and to the ministry of the word."

That day he told me that he would start paying my salary every month so I could remain in the place of prayer. False-humility would have resisted this gift, but I knew God was using Russ in a powerful way. In fact, God understands how important financial ministers are in the church—and so does the enemy.

After some time had passed, I was at the church with a small group of mostly young people. They were talking about their desire to attend onething, IHOPKC's annual conference in Kansas City. They all said that they felt God wanted them to go, but they just didn't have any money at all to pay for gas, food and a hotel room.

In the middle of this conversation, in walks Russ. You couldn't miss Russ when he entered a room. He cruised up on his Harley and made a grand entrance like he always did—not showy, mind you, but here was just something about the way he carried his self.

He interrupted our small gathering and said, "God sent me here tonight because he said there are some people who need money." In typical Russ fashion, he didn't mince words. People were just looking at each other quite shocked that he just so happened to mention what we had been talking about. Was it a coincidence? Of course not.

Though it was clear that God had put it on Russ' heart to give, he needed the people on the other side of the equation to make their case known. Nobody did. I jumped in and boldly said, "Listen everybody, this is a key part of Russ' ministry. Don't dishonor that, and don't lie by refusing to admit what you very well know is true! If you need money, be honest and tell him!"

At that point, I walked out of the room to attend to something. When I got back, Russ was gone—but he didn't leave before he gave a few hundred dollars to each of the people in need. They now had what they needed to go to the conference.

Remember above that I said that both God and the enemy understand the value and power of Kingdom giving? Well, that was the last time I ever saw Russ. One night shortly after, we were watching the news and a story came on that shocked us to the core. Russ had died in an airplane crash.

At his memorial service I was blown away at the number of people and ministries he had been supporting. He literally caused ministry dreams to be fulfilled through his faithful, selfless giving.

God has people like Russ ready for you to contact.

Just a Few Specifics

With that in mind, let's talk specifics. It's common for people to get hung up at this point. They feel led to launch into ministry, but they don't know how to handle various legalities in order to make it official.

First, as I shared in a previous chapter, absolutely do not delay as you wait for all of the specifics to come together. We started Revival Church with a simple prayer meeting. We met and prayed and had church! People initially gave without any expectation of receiving a tax-deduction.

That being said, be sure you consider the laws of your city or county. For example, it's a zone violation to hold meetings in your home in some areas. If that's the case, look for a conference room in a hotel or even a side room at a restaurant! Just be sure you cover your legal bases, but don't presume them to be insurmountable—they aren't!

Our first organizational steps were to setup a board, develop bylaws (which can be obtained online and modified to meet your specific situation) become incorporated and establish a new checking account for Revival Church. We could then start receiving tithes and offerings, and people were eligible to receive a tax-deduction.

While we later did setup a 501c3, which took several months and around $750, it's not necessary to do so before you receive donations. Organizations that meet the necessary criteria to be identified as a church are automatically tax-exempt and givers can also claim donations on their taxes.

Other ministries (non-church) are setup a bit differently and you will want to do some research to learn just what is required before you can receive donations that would be considered tax-deductible for your givers.

The point? It is a piece of cake to start your ministry! Don't let fear stop you from stepping out. As you develop, you can connect with others who can counsel you in the details that need to be addressed.

This book isn't meant to provide legal advice, but rather its an exhortation to respond to the call of God on your life with expediency!

Chapter Eleven
Find Your Tribe

You might find it interesting that this chapter is near the end of the book instead of the beginning. The type of aggressive action that I am promoting usually requires that you identify your tribe after the journey has begun. They will appear in the midst of your adventure, not before it begins.

When we started our churches, we didn't have a launch team. We didn't have anybody other than our own family and whoever chose to show up to the initial meetings. Whether there was nobody but our family, or a room full of expectant people didn't matter. We were launching, and we'd find those who would run with us as time went by.

The risk in this approach is that you will attract people that enjoy your culture, or come alive in your atmosphere, but, after further review, may not truly embrace your core values. They may not have your DNA.

That's OK, and they can certainly be a meaningful part of your venture, but they cannot make up your core leadership team. This is a very important point. Do NOT be tempted to put warm bodies into position prematurely. When they sense that their spiritual genetic code doesn't fit with yours, the result is a divided team instead of a unified one.

I will be the first to admit that this is much easier said than done. I have had really wonderful people in the wrong positions, and have had to pay dearly for it.

I would strongly encourage you to avoid giving titles to anybody for an extended period of time. I don't think it would be unreasonable to wait a year or more before doing so. Give people functions and responsibilities, and you will see how much they come alive in those roles, and how they do or don't support the greater vision of the church or ministry. If they come alive in their role, but can't support the ministry vision well, you will not want to entitle them. Giving titles can result in entitlement in the immature. Entitlement can bring trouble, even if it is completely unintentional.

You will find your tribe most easily in the prayer room. I have yet to find a better way to determine who is and who is not fully on board with you. Develop a fiery prayer culture and gather together continually to cry out to God. Those who are burning with your vision will be obvious—not after one or two prayer meetings, but after a hundred or so.

When you are confident you have people from your tribe on your team, you will be able to move forward with exacting unity and strategic momentum.

When in Colorado we were in need of some help on our staff, so we started a search for someone to fit that position. A man and a wife were recommended to us and we scheduled an interview with them. During the interview both my wife and I felt like they could fit the role well, but I had a slight check in my spirit.

I ignored the check.

My church split.

Allow me to fill in the blanks. After we hired them, they immediately dove into their new position with passion, and did a remarkable job developing it. They were self starters and really did remove a lot of burden off of me and helped the church jump into a small growth spurt.

Every Sunday they would stand by the front door of the church and warmly welcome people with handshakes and hugs. I remember that vividly. Little did I know that this individual and his wife were stealing the hearts of people who were under my care. The Absalom story in scripture was unfolding in my church and I had no idea it was happening.

I discuss the Absalom spirit in my book *Covens in the Church*, and I recommend you study it intently. Absalom stood at the city gates and entertained complaints against his father David, and in doing so stole the hearts of the people.

As I said before, the best way to know who is and who is not with you is to hold white hot prayer meetings. This story is where I discovered the power of this strategy.

I felt a significant attack of witchcraft coming against me one day, though I didn't know where it was coming from. Understand, gossip is witchcraft. It's rebellion. I now know that I was sensing powerful gossip coming against me, and I was actually going to ask someone who was a significant player in the drama of murmuring to help me break that spirit off of the church!

I called my staff together, including the man we had recently hired, and explained that I felt a strong attack of witchcraft coming against me, and that I needed all of us to pray together in the opposing spirit–a spirit of unity. I truly had no idea where the attack was coming from, but I knew what strategy I needed to implement.

I instructed everybody to pray boldly in tongues, and everybody locked in and burned hot in Spirit-driven prayer–except for that man. He looked awkward as he walked around with his arms half raised, feeling fully uncomfortable. You see, praying in the Holy Spirit in unity with those you are divided with is impossible!

The rest of us did pray in power and God did move, though I didn't realize how severe that move would be.

Shortly after that prayer meeting, I received a sudden email from our husband and wife team. They resigned. I was shocked! I really didn't know there was anything wrong, and this information was a surprise indeed.

I requested a meeting, and they declined. They convinced about one fourth of our church body to leave with them. They started their own church and it lasted just several weeks. They then moved back to Florida to the town they lived in before moving to Colorado–and left a bunch of broken, confused people to waste away.

I should have listened to the check in my spirit during their interview. I should also have refused to promote people I didn't know into such a place of authority so quickly.

They weren't a part of our tribe. They didn't have our DNA. They didn't support our vision. They had their own agenda. That is a recipe for disaster, and it certainly was for us.

On the contrary, when you do find people who are truly a part of your tribe, they will stay with you through every struggle, weak moment, failure and trial. Those are the people you want running close with you.

Now, it is important that I make a point here. Different projects require different types and levels of response. Starting a church will demand that you find your tribe. Starting a short-term project may not require that are so exclusive. You will want to analyze your needs and the risks associated with assigning various types of people. Some tasks may safely assigned to those who aren't invested into your vision, while others certainly cannot be.

In a church setting, a worship leader, for example, must embrace your vision while in a business setting a sound engineer or a receptionist may simply need to support it.

The message I'm trying to convey is simple–know your tribe and know what risks are associated with running with those, at any level, who are not a part of it. Also, dream big when you find those in your tribe who are ready to run hard and strong with you!

Chapter Twelve
Just Do It

By now you have a really good idea of the importance of getting the job done. Fervency and urgency must be branded on your spirit. You will find a myriad of excuses not to advance, and most of the excuses are minor, and they delay you only for a short time—until the excuses add up, and show up one after another.

What possibly could have been a fulfilled mission is now not even an initiated mission.

When you have an impression from the Lord that you are to dive into a new initiative, you just have to do it. I will almost always do something concrete when I feel the Lord leading me into something. I may buy a domain name that very day that I can attach to a new website. I may start designing that website that day as well. I may email a few people and cast the vision to them. I sometimes outline it or write an article or create a video.

What has that simple strategy resulted in? Several domains and websites that are no longer functioning, several initiatives that are currently dormant and a small number of healthy, thriving projects. Remember, the goal isn't to avoid failure! Expect failure! In fact, learn to challenge the threat of failure. Move ahead in the difficult, threatening challenges and challenge them right back with ferocity and fearlessness! Expect success! For every success you may fail a hundred times or more, but it is well worth it. Of course, you can use wisdom and minimize the cost of failure. We all have limited emotional energy and finances, so we must consider those limits.

As an example, if I had an extra million dollars laying around, I might buy a thousand web domains, develop sites on a few of them and watch 900 fail, and another 80 or 90 get sold for more than I bought them for. Without a million dollars at my disposal, my investment will be smaller, but I will still be advancing with the understanding that much failure will come and some success will be found as well.

How many tons of dirt do treasure hunters have to dig up before they find gold? How hard do baseball players have to practice for just one shot that may or may not come to play in the major leagues? You get the point.

Firetimes

Right when I was coming alive in ministry, as a young, green, raw man of God, I had the apostolic fires burning in my bones (though I had no idea what apostolic even meant!).

I was already giving some leadership to a youth ministry in Dayton, Ohio that I had a lot of vision for, but there was more in me! I decided to start a ministry with nobody to do it with me except my girlfriend, and no place to meet, except a park. I called it Firetimes.

It was pretty embarrassing, but it was also exhilarating! My girlfriend at the time (my wife now!) gathered some of her friends and we'd meet each week in a park with a boom box and we'd blast worship music as we walked around and prayed with passion! We'd then come together for some open air preaching.

It was a short term success, or a long term failure (depending on how you look at it!), but I look back at that as a key step for me personally. I just did it! Success or failure didn't matter. Why? It wasn' in the equation because I was simply doing what was in me. It was as natural as breathing.

Do you have a potentially embarrassing yet key ministry or project to launch? Will you look back twenty years from now with a cool little story like this to mark your progress, or will fear of failure or nervousness about the bigger picture hold you back? I challenge you to just do it!

Chapter Thirteen
Endure!

Your adventure will be long and extremely hard—if it's worthy of your passion and investment.

One of the most important prophetic words I've ever received came to me when I was visiting IHOPKC many years ago. It was a sudden, unplanned prophetic word that caught me by surprise. The person who gave the word didn't know who I was or what I was involved with in ministry. He looked at me and I could sense it was a very clear, sharp word that he had received. He said this, "If what you are contending for isn't fulfilled for 20 years, will you still contend?"

What was so powerful wasn't the word, it was my response. A few years prior my reaction would have probably been negative. That word would have frustrated me. But, that wasn't my feeling that day. Instantly I came alive with faith coursing through me. I immediately thought to myself, "Of course, that's my calling. What else would I do?" The call to endurance was confirmed in my spirit.

Today, as an aggressive, passionate, apostolic leader, I am settled with the possibility that I may not see fulfillment of my various missions in my lifetime—and I'm fully OK with that. I have eternity on my mind. While I will work as if the mission must be completed tomorrow, I won't become emotionally disengaged if it takes decades.

I think this is part of the reason I feel so strongly about writing articles and books. They will outlast me. My advice? Live for what will outlast you. Put your hand to that plow.

> Daniel 4:34 …for his dominion is an everlasting dominion,
> and his kingdom endures from generation to generation;

God has put eternity into us, and we will forever be a part of his mission, from generation to generation! Ask yourself this question:

Is what you are doing right now going to have impact ten million years from now?

The answer to that question will help you pace yourself with endurance, whether your project is short or long term. The question is about its and your enduring impact.

Final Thoughts
You Can Do It!

My heart is to see people break free from fear as they aggressively and joyfully work towards fulfilling the missions that God has called them to steward.

You really can do it! Whether its starting a church, launching an online ministry, starting a business, writing a book or anything else, if God called you, you can't lose!

Note, I didn't say you can't fail. You will fail. But failing and losing are unrelated. You only lose if you quit.

I would love to hear about your endeavors and both successes and failures. What did you learn? What was harder than you thought or easier than you thought? What was surprising? What was disappointing?

Contact me via my website at johnburton.net. I can't wait to hear your stories and celebrate with you!

CONTACT

John Burton
john**burton**.net

RESOURCES

B Drive Master Collection
 of John's books PLUS MUCH MORE!
ER **120** RESOURCES!

OOKS in printed and ebook format
RDER TODAY!
NBURTON.NET/RESOURCES

John has written several
books that will result
in an awakened spirit,
passion for revival and
a determination to fulfill
your calling!

You are sure to be
marked by the fire of
God as you read!

You can stay connected to the
ministry by subscribing to his email
updates.JOHNBURTON.NET/SUBSCRIBE.

Made in the USA
Charleston, SC
07 August 2013